Look at Me

You can read more stories about
the gang from Buffin Street by
collecting the rest of the series.

For complete list, look at
the back of the book.

Look at Me

Francesca Simon

Illustrated by Emily Bolam

Orion
Children's Books

Look at Me first appeared in *Miaow Miaow Bow Wow*
first published in Great Britain in 2000
by Orion Children's Books
This edition first published in Great Britain in 2012
by Orion Children's Books
a division of the Orion Publishing Group Ltd
Orion House
5 Upper St Martin's Lane
London WC2H 9EA
An Hachette UK Company

1 3 5 7 9 10 8 6 4 2

Text copyright © Francesca Simon 2000, 2012
Illustrations copyright © Emily Bolam 2000

ISBN 978 1 4440 0468 7

Printed in China

BUFFIN STREET

Hello from everyone

Woof

Honey

Miaow

Flick

on Buffin Street

Caw Caw

Do-Re-Mi

Miaow

Lola

Woof

Fang

Snuffle
snuffle

Lily

Miaow

Kit

Bow wow

Prince

Rustle
rustle

Jogger

Growl

Sour Puss

Bow wow

Dizzy

 Miaow

Millie

 Squeak Squeak

Doris Boris

Miaow

Joey

Welcome to Buffin Street!

Come and join all the Buffin Street
dogs, cats, rabbits, puppies and parrots,
and find out what *really* goes on when
their people are out of sight…

Do-Re-Mi brought great
news to Buffin Street.
"Foxham Pond's frozen over!
Foxham Pond's frozen over!"
she squawked.

"Says who?" asked Prince.

"The ducks!" said Do-Re-Mi.
"And they should know."

"Yippee!" said Fang.

"Yippee!" echoed Honey.

Then she stopped.
"What's so great about that?"

"Come on, Honey!" said Millie.
"We're going skating!"

"Skating?" said Honey.

"Skating?" said Honey.
She'd never been skating before
and wasn't sure if she wanted to.

"Don't worry, you'll love it,"
said Millie.

Late that night the animals slipped
out into the cold, frosty darkness.
Buffin Street was silver and silent,
dusted in snow.

Carefully they crossed the road,
trotted past the dry cleaners,
the corner shop, the church and
the playground and scampered
into the park.

There was Foxham Pond,
a gleaming sheet of ice.

"Let's go, Honey!"
shouted Millie.

She bounded onto the ice, whizzing
and whirling with the others.

Honey stared at the twirling skaters.

Then, carefully, she put
her front paws onto the ice.
Brrr! It was cold.

She slid out one paw and skidded.
Whoops!

Honey tried again.
Whoops!
And again.

Suddenly Honey started
sliding across the ice.

"Look out! I can't stop!"
she shouted.

Crash!

"Watch where you're going!"
spat Sour Puss.

"Sorry," said Honey.

This wasn't fun at all.
Fang hurtled by.
"I'm the best! I'm the best skater
in the world," shouted Fang.
Round and round he whizzed.

"Wheee!
Look at me!"
shouted Fang.
"I'm amazing!"

Honey turned away and limped off
the ice, slipping and sliding.

"I don't want to skate any more,"
said Honey.

Fang could zoom about and
she couldn't even get four paws
on the ice without falling.

Someone flashed by.
It was Prince.
Fang stopped skating
and stared.

Prince swooped and looped
and whirled and twirled.

"Wow, look at Prince," said Honey.

Fang turned away.
"Huh," he said. "What a show-off.
I'm tired of skating anyway.
I'm going home."

"Wheee!
Look at me!"
shouted Prince,
prancing and dancing.
"I'm amazing!"

Someone else flashed by.
It was Millie.
Prince stopped skating
and stared.

Millie be-bopped and hopped,
shimmied and streaked.

Honey could not believe her eyes.
"Wow, look at Millie," she said.

Prince turned up his nose
and walked off the ice.

"Wheee!
Look at me!"
shouted Millie.
"I'm amazing!"

Honey sat for a moment.
Then she got up and walked
onto the ice.

Wobble...

Whoops!

Down she crashed.

She got to her feet and tried again.

Wobble...

Wobble...

Whoops!

And then . . .

Wobble . . .

Wobble...

Wheeeeeeeeeee!

She was gliding. She was sliding.
And she wasn't falling.
She was skating!

"Wheee!
Look at me!"
shouted Honey.
"I'm amazing!"

Woof woof
follow me

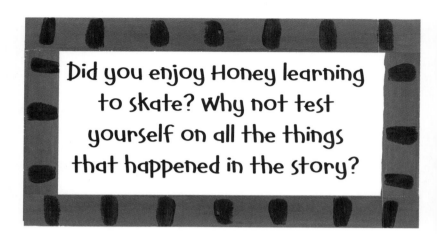

Did you enjoy Honey learning to skate? Why not test yourself on all the things that happened in the story?

What is the great news Do-Re-Mi brings to Buffin Street?

Who invites Honey to go skating?

What happens when Honey first steps
onto the ice?

Who tells Honey to watch where she's going?

Who thinks he is the best skater in the world?

Who swoops and loops and whirls and twirls on the ice?

What does Millie do on the ice?

What does Honey shout when
she skates?

For more adventures with the
Buffin Street Gang, look out for
the other books in the series.

Meet
the Gang

Yum Yum

Rampage in Prince's Garden

Jogger's Big Adventure

The Haunted House of Buffin Street

Miaow Miaow Bow Wow